THE GLOBAL WAR ON TERRORISM: AMERICA'S JIHAD

In the aftermath of the September 11 attacks on the World Trade Center and the Pentagon, President George W. Bush declared the strikes by Al Qaeda were "more than acts of terror. They were acts of war."[1] An unscrupulous enemy had attacked the shores of the United States, killed innocent civilians, and provoked our entry into a struggle which would be cast as the global war on terrorism (GWOT). This phrase would prove to be far more than a bumper sticker response to communicate a theme to an anxious public. GWOT would prove to be a battle cry to a wide spectrum of audiences, both home and abroad, and it would frame an agenda that would lead the United States into a perpetual struggle against a form of radical Islam that is not bounded by the borders of a nation state or organized under the flag of a recognized national capitol.

The Bush administration's global war on terrorism strategy aspired to galvanize Americans and foreign allies against a common enemy, but the high costs of implementing the strategy have subjected GWOT to criticism and controversy. Over the past six years the administration has been under constant pressure from divisive political foes, disenfranchised international allies, questioning legal scholars, unrelenting media interests, and an impatient and fearful public. Under the banner of GWOT the nation has plunged into war in Iraq and Afghanistan while simultaneously beginning a process of restructuring its homeland security apparatus, transforming its military, modifying its privacy laws and civil liberties, and re-assessing its international alliances and allegiances. If U.S. citizens accept that the global war on terrorism is a war unlike any other, then they must also accept responsibility to review the effort and determine whether the wide ranging costs are commensurate with the investment. In doing so, America will reconcile its struggle with terrorism in the context of policies historically defined against the backdrop of conventional war. The nation thus determines whether the opportunity costs associated with prosecution of the global war on terrorism are effectively securing the homeland, or marginalizing traditional national values.

This research project examines key U.S. government and Bush administration, policy and strategy decisions in a complex struggle that has been defined as the global war on terrorism. The project assesses its significance as a strategic and doctrinal framework, and its impacts on U.S. foreign policy and civil liberties.

'War' as a Strategy

Defining war has been a pursuit of military and political science theorists since Sun Tzu first began to articulate military strategy over 2,500 years ago. The most widely accepted modern definition was proposed by the great Prussian scholar of war, Carl von Clausewitz. Clausewitz's signature thesis stated that when communities go to war, the reasons always lie in some manifestation of a political situation. "War therefore is an act of policy...Policy will permeate military operations.[2] As an extension of policy, war thus becomes justification for the use of military force in the pursuit of national strategy or policy.

The notion that the global war on terrorism is a war, (albeit a different kind of war), was brought to the nation's attention by President Bush during what is widely regarded as his most effective address to a joint session of Congress and the American people, nine days after the attacks of 9/11. During the course of his speech Bush stressed that an "act of war" was committed against the country and that the enemy was an organization of al Qaeda related terrorists practicing a form of Islamic extremism directly at war with American freedoms. President Bush continued to state that as a matter of policy, America would fight and win this war through every diplomatic, intelligence, law enforcement, and financial resource available. He added that the nation would direct "every necessary weapon of war to the disruption and to the defeat of the global terror network."[3] Bush was careful to remind his audience that the war would be a lengthy struggle that would include both overt and covert manifestations, seen and unseen by the public. He asked the American people for their patience in a persistent campaign that would not end "with a decisive liberation of territory and a swift conclusion."[4] In his words, it would be a struggle "unlike any we have ever seen...a task that does not end."[5]

In the case of the GWOT, history professor Michael Howard suggests that the Bush administration stumbled upon the phrase when Secretary of State Colin Powell first declared that the United States was at war with terrorism in the immediate aftermath of the September 11 attacks. He further states that Powell made "a very natural but terrible and irrevocable error."[6] Howard's claim is a popular one that the term war is only reasonable if used in the same sense as the war on drugs, or the war on crime. In that context, GWOT would denote the necessity to apply all available resources against what could be deemed "a dangerous, antisocial activity, one that can never be entirely eliminated but can be reduced to, and kept at, a level that does not threaten social stability."[7] By Howard's definition, terrorists are criminals, not to be dignified with the status of belligerents. In his view, the misuse of 'war' is more than a matter of legality or semantics. GWOT is a term that creates an expectation of "spectacular military action" as the first, vice the last resort.[8]

Academics like George Lakoff of the Rockridge Institute have criticized the global war on terrorism term based on the definition of terrorism itself. Lakoff argues that "there can not literally be a war on terror, since terror is an abstract."[9] These critics surmise that if terrorism is a tactic or a method of using violence to further the political agenda of an irregular group, then it is folly to go to war against an enemy identified not by their desired ends, but by their ways. Retired U.S. ambassador Ronald Spiers states that the war on terrorism "is a war without an end in sight, without an exit strategy, with enemies specified not by their aims but by their tactics."[10] Writing for *The Nation*, William Greider offers that the war on terrorism is a politically useful term for the Bush administration, but irrational for the nation. Spiers claims the use of GWOT as a label preyed on the public's growing fear of possible threats and dangers, thus enabling an environment where the President could commit a vast array of the nation's resources and energies towards confronting an unseen enemy.[11]

In opposition to these critics of both the terminology and the premise of the GWOT, few have proven to be as influential in arguing the merits and necessity of the Bush administration's global war on terrorism as law professor and former Department of Justice, Office of Legal Counsel, attorney John Yoo. From 2001 to 2003 Yoo argued the case for war on behalf of the administration, and more recently outlined his reasoning in his 2006 book titled, *War by Other Means*. While Yoo acknowledges the viewpoint that terrorism has previously been recognized by the U.S. judicial system as a criminal act, Yoo posits that the organizational scope of al Qaeda, the deliberate level of planning, financing and execution, and the sheer scale of destruction caused by a foreign organization with political motives, unequivocally started a war between al Qaeda and the United States. Yoo clarifies that the global war on terrorism is aimed at the al Qaeda movement specifically, and points out that the organization can not be eliminated as a threat to the security of the U.S. through the use of inadequate criminal justice approaches, but must be underpinned with the special powers of war to prevent future attacks on their citizens. Yoo references the September 18, 2001, Congressional enactment of an Authorization for Use of Military Force as evidence of a "declaration of war in purpose."[12] Yoo points to the Congressional pronouncement that the attacks of September 11 were, "grave acts of violence" that "pose unusual and extraordinary threat to the national security and foreign policy of the United States."[13] By Yoo's assessment the United States is involved in an international armed conflict with al Qaeda "that is a different kind of war, with a slippery enemy that has no territory, population, or uniformed, traditionally organized armed forces...new enemies of the twenty-first century."[14]

The message transmitted by the global war on terrorism theme has been criticized from left leaning opponents like former North Carolina Senator, John Edwards who claims that the Bush administration misused "[GWOT] doctrine like a sledgehammer to justify the worst abuses and biggest mistakes...from Guantanamo to Abu Graib, to the war in Iraq."[15] Critics like Edwards see GWOT as a misplaced theme in pursuit of long-standing policy objectives to invade Iraq. Supporters on the right like senior North Carolina Senator Elizabeth Dole, prefer to view GWOT as a justifiable framework under which to best mobilize the nation's resources. In Dole's view GWOT is a struggle very much like the Cold War, where Ronald Reagan's resolve in the face of criticism pursued a vision that ended the global threat of communism. Dole states unequivocally that "we cannot cut and run – we know all too well what is at stake in this global war on terror."[16] Perhaps former neo-conservative Pentagon advisor Richard Perle characterized the issue appropriately when he stated that the GWOT message sends a mixed signal because it "has not succeeded in inspiring the belief that we face an existential threat...the term 'war on terrorism' leaves the enemy ill defined."[17]

Reviewing the past six years of American policy in the prosecution of GWOT and assessing whether application of the terminology of GWOT has had a positive strategic effect on the desired end state, or whether it remains relevant, is at the center of the debate. Whether the perception is favorable or negative, references to GWOT have sustained traction with an international audience. John Judis, senior editor at the New Republic, states that the term 'war' was strategically correct in Afghanistan where the Taliban government was deposed and al Qaeda suffered significant set-backs as a result of lost sanctuary and key leadership. Judis continues, however, to state that the global war on terrorism acquired "so much political weight that it endures well after its meaning has exhausted."[18] Judis' viewpoint is not without relevance to the Bush administration. The Bush team continues to pursue al Qaeda in part with the military element of national power, but they too have made attempts to soften the wartime rhetoric. In July of 2005 the *Herald Tribune* reported that the Bush administration was "retooling its slogan for the fight against al Qaeda" as a "global struggle against violent extremism" or GSAVE, vice the global war on terrorism. The stated purpose for the change in terminology reportedly grew out of advice from senior national security advisors, and "reflect[ed] the evolution in Bush's own thinking nearly four years after the

September 11 attacks."[19] Regardless of the Bush administration's motive, the change

from GWOT to GSAVE never gained traction with the U.S. public. In December of

2006, in the wake of a conscious decision by the British Foreign Office to stop using the

global war on terror term, British media were reporting that "President Bush continues to

employ the [GWOT] liberally." The British view is particularly salient because it

highlights the importance that U.S. leadership means to America's most reliable ally in

the GWOT. The British view identifies what could be described as an egregious

oversight by the Bush administration that only made international coalition building more

difficult. More than a year later, the 'global war on terrorism' is standard terminology

found in the executive summary of the official White House progress report on

terrorism.[20] In the UK, popular support for GWOT is waning.

Identifying America's struggle against al Qaeda and Islamic extremism through

the prism of 'war' has proven to be a controversial strategy. In the view of Professor

Samantha Power of the Kennedy School of Government at Harvard, "most Americans

still rightly believe that the United States must confront Islamic terrorism…but Bush's

premises have proved flawed, and the war on terror has obscured more than it has

clarified."[21] Power's assessment is that GWOT gave birth to an agenda that needlessly

dismissed old rules of criminal justice, setback US diplomatic relationships with allies,

exploited international treaties and organizations, and led to dramatic expansions of

Presidential power.[22] Countering viewpoints are supported by actual facts that show

some levels of progress as a result of U.S. actions. The counter argument is made by

the Bush administration in the *White House Progress Report on the Global War on*

Terrorism, where readers are reminded that since 9/11 al Qaeda has been denied sanctuary in Afghanistan, two thirds of the senior al Qaeda leaders under observation by the US have been apprehended or killed, terrorist cells in numerous US cities have been disrupted, and nearly $200 million have been denied to terror networks.[23]

The premise that the global war on terrorism is a 'war' is a subject of debate that provides compelling arguments from all sides of the issue. The enemy is a non-state entity who resists through both asymmetric and irregular methods is forcing scholars of war to reassess doctrine and determine whether there is room for such an untidy arrangement. Claims that the GWOT mantra is a means to consolidate power and influence, and promote the policy aims of the administration is evidenced in significant levels of expansion of executive branch wartime powers. The credibility of the GWOT campaign is supported by the Bush administration's leveraging the instruments of war through a legitimate combination of public support, congressional funding, and judicial approval.

A Case for Preemption

The strategic policy of preemptive wartime doctrine has come under scrutiny by international legal scholars like Richard Falk of Princeton University, who states that Bush's doctrine "claims the right to abandon rules of restraint and law patiently developed over the course of centuries…permit[ing] states to use force non-defensively against their enemies…creating a terrible precedent."[24] Despite the criticism and controversy, the case for preemptive war is made clear in the National Security Strategy of the United States of America for 2006. In the document, the Bush administration reiterates the strategy of 2002 and states that in order to meet its obligation to protect the American people and American interests, the government is obligated to "use all elements of national power, before the threats can do grave damage."[25] While the text further states that the preference will always be for non-military actions to succeed first, the policy is clear in its presumption that there exist few options for preempting a potential terrorist attack with WMD, than preemption and action.[26] This policy of preemption, often identified as the center-piece of the so called "Bush Doctrine," has served as a rallying point for critics and supporters from both ends of the political and ideological spectrum to speculate as to the legality, the advisability, and the context of preemption as policy.[27]

Noted defense strategist Colin Gray, a dual citizen of and advisor to both U.S. and British governments, makes a distinction between preemption and prevention, stating that preemption has never been a questionable issue either morally or legally. Gray states that preemption, as defined by policy strategists, is "to launch an attack against an attack that one has incontrovertible evidence is either actually underway or has been ordered."[28] Gray states that preemption was a widely understood by the United Nations as an acceptable concept during the Cold War, referring to the first use of force in the face of an imminent enemy attack. Gray bluntly claims that preemption is related directly to self defense.[29] Prevention, on the other hand, is the issue Gray perceives to be at the heart of the GWOT example, and what the Bush administration actually refers to when it calls for "the occasional necessity for preemption."[30] The fundamental difference is that launching a preventive war or a preventive strike must be based on a "specific purpose of forestalling an extraordinary danger."[31] In Gray's opinion, preventive war is a "frightening concept" that can realistically be waged by strong states, but must be used judiciously.[32] Gray perceives as reasonable, the contention that "because the United States has an extraordinary responsibility for maintaining world order, it is permitted to act, indeed it sometimes has to act, in ways that would be unacceptable if practiced by others."[33]

Austrian President of the International Progress Organization, Dr. Hans Koechler, scorns the Bush administration for its application of preemptive war in Iraq as undermining international law and the authority of the United Nations. Koechler contends that preemptive action by the U.S., in the absence of UN Security Council approval, establishes a dangerous precedent under which other nations could justify unprovoked invasions of other states.[34] Koechler posits that "preventive war, as advanced in the new strategic doctrine of the United States, is not in any way compatible with the United Nations Charter."[35] Koechler claims that U.S. policies since 9/11 have served to undermine the international rule of law as well as the multilateral international order advocated by the UN. Koechler states that the U.S., acting in its role as sole superpower, "arrogates itself the right to act on behalf of mankind – a right that is …exclusively reserved to the Security Council."[36] At its worst, Koechler fears that the national sovereignty of states guaranteed by UN charter have been "reduced to a state's freedom to define itself vis-à-vis the only superpower."[37] Those states are therefore subjected to the notion of being with, or against the world's superpower, and in the process falling into the hegemon's definition of good or evil.[38]

Whether a policy of preemption, (or preventive war), by the U.S. is deemed questionable under UN charter, justifiable in the context of an emerging twenty-first century terrorist threat, or even desirable policy in coalition building, the conventional wisdom among supporters of preemption remains that preventive war is a strategy that must be used selectively, and likely resides only with the great world powers.[39] Supporters of the Bush policy refer to the convoluted actions of the UN as their credibility. In the aftermath of the 9/11 attacks, the UN Security Council issued a resolution recognizing the United States' right of self defense against a terrorist threat. The UN defined the terrorist actions as "a threat to international peace and security."[40] The UN's International Court of Justice did not accept the concept that non-state actors have become purveyors of 'war' against sovereign nations.[41] UN actions that tend to contradict themselves serve to discredit the organization in the eyes of many member nations, and are typically cause for the U.S. to question the authority of an organization whose members typically have proportionally less responsibility for global security than the world's sole superpower.

Many nations interpret the UN charter as a legal document that restricts the actions to wage preventive war without the blessing of the United Nation's Security Council (UNSC). The Bush administration rejected this interpretation in favor of the right to defend its citizens against a potential terrorist threat that could lead to mass casualties many times greater than the attacks of 9/11.[42] This Bush interpretation supports the concept that the U.S. has the right to take active measures in the interest of its security. The Bush concept discounts the validity of the Security Council to interpret U.S. actions legally or morally when each of the permanent members has its own security interests at the forefront of any issue on which they vote.[43]

Prior to the invasion of Iraq, liberal political activist Ralph Nader was one of the most vocal public figures to suggest that the Bush administration's argument for the invasion of Iraq had little to do with the pretext of pursuing GWOT. Nader highlighted

flimsy intelligence assessments and a questionable terrorist nexus as flawed

justification for the invasion of Iraq.[44] Nader predicted the invasion of Iraq would

"increase global terrorism...destabilize the Middle East region, undermine [GWOT] and

distract from the Israeli – Palestinian conflict."[45] Initially discounted in mainstream

politics as a radical, Nader's opinions have gained increasing credibility as the invasion

into Iraq brought more terrorism into the region and reportedly emboldened the

recruiting efforts of the al Qaeda movement.[46] In February of 2007, *The Independent*

reported results of a study by Peter Bergen and Paul Cruickshank that highlight U.S.

strategy failures validated by the U.S. government's own 2006 National Intelligence

Estimate (NIE) on GWOT. The report states that "the Iraq war has become the 'cause

célèbre' for jihadists...shaping a new generation of terrorist leaders."[47] The NIE asserts

that the perceived unjustified invasion into a WMD free Iraq has had a significant effect

in radicalizing Muslim fundamentalists. Bergen and Cruickshank cite that the worldwide

death toll at the hands of terrorists rose from 729 to 5,420 in the three years following

the invasion of Iraq versus the three years prior to the invasion.[48]

In January of 2007, John Negroponte, the Director of National Intelligence,

downplayed the NIE stating that he "wouldn't say there has been widespread growth in

Islamic extremism beyond Iraq."[49] Supporters of the war in Iraq, like Jeffrey Bell and

Frank Cannon of the conservative Washington consulting firm, Capital City Partners,

view the growth of terrorist activity inside Iraq as an indicator that the war in Iraq

remains the central battlefield in GWOT. Bell and Cannon state that Bush was right

when he "concluded that nothing less than a democratic revolution in the Arab world stood any chance of removing the roots of terrorism."[50] Bell and Cannon point to the growth of terrorism in Iraq as proof that al Qaeda leaders fear that the potential democratization of Iraq would be devastating to the their cause.[51] The March 2006 National Security Strategy is prescient in its assessment that "terrorists today see Iraq as the central front in their fight against the United States...the success of democracy in Iraq will be a launching pad for freedom's success throughout [the] region."[52] History will look back at the invasion of Iraq and allow for an informed assessment based on the existence of a democratic or an extremist state. While precise terminology is important to policy makers and diplomats, U.S. GWOT strategy is less likely to be judged through the context U.S. political elections or international debates over the nuances of preemptive versus preventive war. Iraq's status as a prominent democracy or an extremist state will eventually be a reflection of the dramatic revolution proposed by Ball and Cannon, or the emboldened enemy as characterized by Nader.

A Strategy of Unilateralism - With Us or Against Us

The significant impacts of prosecuting GWOT can be seen in wide ranging effects on traditional American values, U.S. military commitment, and international relations. Critics of the war effort, like former National Security Advisor Zbigniew Brzezinski, cite grievances in long lists of consequences and costs to American ideals and global leadership.[53] Critics like Brzezinski perceive the marginalization of American values and international standing far outweighs the strategies and policies brought to bear as part of GWOT. Those in support of GWOT, like conservative consultants Bell and Cannon view America's unilateral approach as inevitable in what they consider to be a bipolar conflict between al Qaeda and the U.S.[54] Expensive as it is, Bell and

Cannon propose that the benefit of GWOT far exceeds the possibility of a "renewed campaign of mass murder on the American mainland."[55]   The United States' policies in the GWOT strategy have had lasting effects that will shape the nation's destiny as a superpower as it navigates the twenty-first century.

Lee Kuan Yew, the former Prime Minister of Singapore, provides an important perspective into America's GWOT policies during an acceptance speech for the Woodrow Wilson Award for Public Service in October 2006. Yew contends that the U.S. abandoned its Cold War successes against the Soviet Union and communism, which were based on inclusiveness, for GWOT policies that have been founded on unilateralism. Yew states that "perceptions of U.S. unilateralism triggered an informal counter coalition of necessity among those countries that oppose the coalition of the willing."[56] Yew stated that most members of the counter coalition were not supporters of jihadists, but America's encroachment caused them to respond in disagreement to protect their own interests. In summary, Yew warns that the "long-term fight against Islamic militants is in its early rounds," but for the U.S. to succeed it will take a wide coalition.[57]

The alienation of traditional allies has been an unfortunate and deleterious result of the global war on terrorism. In his book, *Winning the Right War*, Phillip Gordon points to the Bush campaign platform of 2000 as an indication of ideology that would become policy. The administration's willingness to act alone through the premise that "U.S. foreign policy goals could only be realized through decisive American leadership and, if necessary, through unilateral action."[58] The problem, according to Gordon, is that after more than six years, the U.S. is standing alone. By "neglecting diplomacy, ignoring the foreign policy priorities of allies…invad[ing] Iraq and accusing opponents of the war of disloyalty," the administration needlessly alienated our traditional allies throughout the world.[59]   A host of Pew Global Attitudes Project surveys show that nations from Eurasia to the Middle East overwhelmingly view the US with a "less than favorable opinion" since prior to 2002.[60]   Nonetheless, neo-conservative supporters of the Bush policy, like Weekly Standard editor William Kristol, conclude that America has national interests at stake that are commensurate with its superpower status. Many, like the conservative Kristol, perceive that U.S. unilateral actions are a sign of strength, and if the downside is that "people want to say we're an imperial power, fine."[61]

Kristol's willingness to accept a unilateral approach as a sign of strength is seen by other strategists, like Director of the Europe Program for the Center for Strategic and International Studies (CSIS), Julianne Smith, as an obstacle to America's ability to address broader global challenges. In a statement before the House Committee on Foreign Affairs, Smith noted that while the Bush administration may be correct in their pronouncement that "making policy is not a popularity contest," the Bush administration fails to take into account that when key political leaders from other countries "feel that standing shoulder to shoulder with the United States is a political liability, low favorability ratings can indeed hinder America's ability to solve global challenges."[62] At the crux of the negative view that exists of America is Washington's unwillingness to grant due process to terrorist suspects, along with violations of human rights during interrogations. Smith warns that European audiences view these issues as the epitome of hypocrisy and proves there is a "gap between U.S. stated policies and action."[63] Smith concludes that there is a case for a revitalization of the war on terror based on America welcoming debate among coalition allies over strategies associated with the GWOT. Key among the initiatives would be a U.S. commitment to human rights in the conduct of counter terrorism.[64] This approach would restore the "moral authority" that Smith claims is "eroding, jeopardizing the transatlantic relationship and threatening U.S. national security."[65]

While the Bush administration freely admits that success requires the "support and concerted action of friends and allies,"[66] the public backing of both traditional and non-traditional allies has been difficult to organize. This leaves the administration with a curious challenge alluded to by President Bush in his letter that opens the 2006 National Security Strategy. If success in confronting the threats and challenges the U.S. faces in GWOT "rests on strong alliances, friendships, and international institutions…in common purpose with others,"[67] then it stands to reason that a reassessment of U.S. strategy is necessary in order to broaden a coalition of those nations perceived as willing, into a coalition of those with shared national interests.

Civil Liberties and the Fear Factor

Controversies on the U.S. home front are as much or more contentious than on the international scene. Reverberations from the global war on terrorism have had a significant impact on executive branch power and civil liberties. In their 2002 book titled *Terrorism and the Constitution*, David Cole and James Dempsey conclude that GWOT requires that the constitutional limits applicable to the U.S. government be at the forefront of all initiatives and that responses be "measured, balanced, and effective," vice what Cole and Dempsey consider to have been "a pattern of overreaction."[68] The centerpiece of Cole and Dempsey's argument is that security, intelligence, and military

16

responses are warranted as the U.S. prosecutes GWOT and pursues al Qaeda. Ccle and Dempsey warn that America should not respond in an environment of excessive fear and "sacrifice the bedrock foundations of our constitutional democracy – political freedom, due process, and equal treatment."[69] According to Cole and Dempsey it is curious irony that America is responding to the terrorist threat by "trampl[ing] the very freedoms we are fighting for."[70]

Legal professor John Yoo views the concessions differently, proposing that the war on terror is a conflict with a foreign enemy who is not a beneficiary of the same peacetime rules that protect American citizens in criminal justice scenarios. Yoo offers that constitutional protections available to Americans within the system are to ensure power is not abused by government. It "involves the fundamental relationship between the people and its government, and so ought to be regulated by clear, strict rules defining the power given by the principal to its agent."[71] Yoo contends that any and all efforts that apply criminal justice rules to al Qaeda associated terrorists and affiliates would both impede the apprehension of the enemy and compromise the necessary secrecy of military initiatives.[72] From Yoo's standpoint, the war on terror is a temporary condition of war that requires extraordinary powers to be in place to efficiently eradicate a threat to the very core of America's existence.

Writing for the Washington Post, Zbigniew Brzezinski claims that GWOT created a culture of fear that has become so elevated that it has had a "pernicious impact on American democracy" which has undermined the nation's ability to face the actual challenges associated with terrorism.[73] According to Brzezinski, the American public has been brainwashed into believing the terrorist threat is so pervasive, that paranoia has developed leading to a level of security procedures that wasted millions of dollars of taxpayer money while "contributing to a siege mentality."[74]

Brzezinski claims that byproducts of this national paranoia are clearly visible in a level of social discrimination and harassment towards Muslims in the U.S. that has harmed America's reputation "as a leader in fostering constructive interracial and interreligious relations."[75] A troubling civil rights scenario has effected the general population, where due process has been marginalized and US citizens apprehended, in an environment where innocent until proven guilty is sacrificed in a futile effort to prevent terrorism while convicting terrorists. Brzezinski appeals to U.S. leadership to "stop this paranoia…even in the face of future terrorist attacks" so that America can "be true to our traditions."[76]

Zbigniew Brzezinski states that traditional civil liberties held by U.S. citizens have been adversely impacted in support of 'war time' security measures, enacted by the government in order to fight terrorist networks. Brzezinski concludes that GWOT accomplished a primary objective of "stimulating the emergence of a culture of fear" which made it easier to garner support for the policies they wanted to pursue.[77]

Key among the policies under the scrutiny of civil libertarians include the USA PATRIOT Act of 2001 and the Bush administration's domestic surveillance program, through which the National Security Agency (NSA) monitors international communications initiated by suspected al Qaeda members and affiliates.[78] While traditional conservatives view these as sacrifices commensurate with a nation at war, President of the International Progress Organization, Hans Koechler, warns that the extreme security measures taken in the name of GWOT threaten the most basic liberties, such as the freedom of expression, freedom of information, and protection of privacy. Koechler concludes that the intensity of the measures taken is more attributable to a totalitarian system than that of the enlightened West.[79] Koechler fears that there is a building pressure in the U.S. for its citizens to come into line with the government's general views about the enemy, marginalizing those who fail to conform.[80] The end result of this panic is a "forcible consensus" on the nation's strategy and policies.[81]

In their recently published book, Terror in the Balance, legal scholars Eric Posner and Adrian Vermeule conclude that the panic thesis held by libertarians, that fear causes government leaders exaggerate threats and neglect traditional civil liberties in order to expand constitutional powers, is wrong.[82]

In the case of the GWOT, Posner and Vermeule posit that libertarians themselves have over-reacted to a perceived threat of civil liberties violations, and underestimated the benefits of government actions taken on behalf of security. The panic exhibited by libertarians in response to government security measures inspired the libertarians to falsely conclude that powers authorized under post 9/11 policies, such as the PATRIOT Act and NSA surveillance measures, are violations of law, when in fact these actions were supported by lawmakers and judges overwhelmingly.[83] In addressing the ultimate value of civil liberties and national values at a time of emergency, Posner and Vermeule surmise that "most people do not want to live in a society that protects civil liberties at an extremely high price" that jeopardizes their security.[84] Posner and Vermeule conclude that it is a fallacy to assume that "whatever package of civil liberties happens to exist at a time a terrorist threat arises must be maintained at all costs...[because] a government that does not respond as a threat increases is "pathologically rigid, not enlightened."[85] In the aftermath of the catastrophic terrorist attacks of 9/11 there is little doubt whether America needed to respond in a lasting and significant way. There is also little doubt that those responses will be reconciled, ensuring their consequences do not go beyond reason in protecting freedom, at the cost of freedom.

Conclusion

The terrorist attacks of 9/11 presented the United States with its greatest challenge since the end of the Cold War. A seemingly invincible sense of national security and safety was shattered by an asymmetric and irregular threat that brought a war to the U.S. home front for which the nation was unprepared. In response, the Bush led government declared the global war on terrorism had commenced against the worst brand of Islamic extremism, led by an al Qaeda master. This 'war' on terrorism is justifiable, and requires the nation's leaders to take aggressive actions to defeat al Qaeda and ensure the safety of U.S. citizens, as well as to protect America's interests abroad. It is reasonable to question the actions taken to date, and to ensure that the framework being established to adapt to these new rules of war does not sacrifice the same freedoms we are attempting to protect. GWOT requires the military instrument be leveraged to take the fight to the enemy on distant battlefields, but it also requires that those battlefields be carefully assessed to ensure the effort does not empower the very enemy we are attempting to eliminate. As the world's sole superpower, the United States must continue to lead against the terrorist scourge, but the U.S. must exhibit as much patience and imagination towards building international consensus and multilateralism, as it does to act alone in the face of indecisiveness and political cowardice. American leadership must not lose sight of the fact that no strategy can be formed without consulting the nation's values. America has the economic and industrial might to erect new buildings, the ingenuity and flexibility to alter its security environment, and the courage and strength to sacrifice its young men and women in the defense of its citizens. However, mortgaging the principles established by the nation's founders in the pursuit of short term gains will result in a series of successful battles, followed by a lost war.

Endnotes

[1] George W. Bush, Address to a Joint Session of Congress and the American People, United States Capitol, Washington D.C., 20 September 2001, linked from *The White House Home Page* at "News Releases," available from http//www.whitehouse.gov/news/releases/2001/09/print/20010920-8.html; Internet; accessed 18 January 2008.

[2] Carl von Clausewitz, *On War*, ed. and trans. Michael Howard and Peter Paret, 2nd ed. (Princeton, NJ: Princeton University Press, 1976), 75.

[3] Bush.

[4] Ibid

[5] Ibid.

[6] Michael Howard, "What's in a Name?: How to Fight Terrorism," *Foreign Affairs* 81, no. 1 (January/February 2002): 8.

[7] Ibid.

[8] Ibid., 9.

[9] "Criticism of the War on Terror" Wikipedia, the free encyclopedia, available from http://en.wikipedia.org/wiki/Criticism_of_the_War_on_Terror; Internet; accessed 23 October 2007.

[10] William Greider, "Under the Banner of the 'War' on Terror," *The Nation*, 21 June 2004; available from http://www.thenation.com/doc/20040621/greider; Internet; accessed 23 October 2007.

[11] Ibid.

[12] John Yoo, *War By Other Means: An Insiders Account of the War on Terror* (New York: Atlantic Monthly Press, 2006), 3-11.

[13] Ibid., 11.

[14] Ibid., 17.

[15] John Edwards, "Bush's Global War on Terror Has Backfired," *Real Clear Politics*, 23 May 2007; available from http://www.realclearpolitics.com/articles/2007/05 /a_strong _military_for_a_ new_ce.html; Internet; accessed 27 February 2008.

[16] Elizabeth Dole, "Dole: Much at Stake in the Global War on Terror," *The Charlotte Observer,* 19 November 2005, available from http://dole.senate.gov/index.cfm?Fuse Action=Articles.Detail&Article_id=37&Month=11; Internet; accessed 27 February 2008.

[17] Guy Raz, "Defining the War on Terror," 23 October 2007, linked from the National Public Radio Home Page at "Middle East," available from http://www.npr.org/templates/story/story.php ?storyId=6416780

[18] John Judis, "What is the War on Terror?" *The New Republic Online*, 5 June 2006; available from http://www.carnegieendowment.org/publications/index.cfm?fa=view&id=18409 &prog=zgp&proj=zusr

[19] Eric Schmidt and Thom Shanker, "Washington Recasts Terror War as Struggle," *International Herald Tribune*, [newspaper on-line]; available from http://www.iht.com/articles /2005/07/26/news/terror.php; Internet; accessed 23 October 2007.

[20] George W. Bush, "Progress Report on the Global War on Terrorism," available from http://www.whitehouse.gov/homeland/progress/summary.html; Internet; accessed 21 January 2008.

[21] Samantha Power, "Our War on Terror," *The New York Times,* 29 July 2007 [newspaper on-line]; available from http://www.nytimes.com/2007/07/29/books/review/Power-t.html?pagewanted=5&_r=1; Internet; accessed 23 October 2007.

[22] Ibid.

[23] Bush, "Progress Report on the Global War on Terrorism," 1.

[24] Richard Falk, "The New Bush Doctrine," *The Nation,* 15 July 2002, available from http://www.thenation.com/doc/20020715/falk; Internet; accessed 28 February 2008.

[25] George W. Bush, *The National Security Strategy of the United States of America*, (Washington, D.C.: The White House, March 2006),18.

[26] Ibid.

[27] Colin S. Gray, *The Implications of Preemptive and Preventive War Doctrines: A Reconsideration*, (Carlisle Barracks, PA: Strategic Studies Institute, July 2007), 1-10.

[28] Ibid., 9.

[29] Ibid., 8-9.

[30] Ibid., 11.

[31] Ibid., 21.

[32] Ibid., 22.

[33] Ibid., 44.

[34] Hans Koechler, "The War on Terror, Its Impact on the Sovereignty of States, and Its Implications for Human Rights and Civil Liberties," 25 September 2002; http://hanskoechler. com/nccp-conf-terrorism-manila2002.html; Internet; accessed 23 October 2008.

[35] Ibid.

[36] Ibid., 3.

[37] Ibid., 5.

[38] Ibid., 5.

[39] Gray, 47-52.

[40] Yoo, 14.

[41] Ibid.

[42] Gray, 33 -35

[43] Ibid.

[44] Ralph Nader, "Pre-emptive War on a Defenseless Country," *Counterpunch Newsletter,* 25 March 2003: available from http://www.counterpunch.org/nader03252003.html.; Internet; accessed 28 February 2008.

[45] Ibid.

[46] Kim Sengupta and Patrick Cockburn, "How the War on Terror Made the World a More Terrifying Place," *The Independent*, 28 February 2007: available from http://news.independent .co.uk/world/middle_east/article2311307.ece; accessed 18 January 2008.

[47] Ibid.

[48] Ibid.

[49] Ibid.

[50] Jeffrey Bell and Frank Cannon, "The War on Terror: Year Five," *Weekly Standard,* 19 August 2005: available from http://www.cbsnews.com/stories/2005/08019/opinion/ printable 788708.shtml; accessed 24 January 2008.

[51] Ibid.

[52] Bush, *The National Security Strategy of the United States of America*, 12-13.

[53] Zbigniew Brzezinski, "Terrorized by the War on Terror," *Washington Post*, 25 March 2007 [newspaper on-line]; available from http://www.washington post.com/wp-yn/content/article/2007/03/23/AR2007032301613; Internet; accessed 23 October 2007.

[54] Bell and Cannon, 1.

[55] Ibid., 2.

[56] Lee Kuan Yew, "The United States, Iraq, and the War on Terror: A Singaporean Perspective," *Foreign Affairs* 86, no. 1 (January/February 2007): 3.

[57] Ibid., 7.

[58] Philip H. Gordon, *Winning the Right War: The Path to Security for America and the World* (New York: Times Books, Henry Holt and Company, 2007), 30.

[59] Ibid., 31.

[60] Ibid., 32-33.

[61] Ibid., 32.

[62] Julianne Smith, "Extraordinary Rendition in U.S. Counter terrorism Policy: The Impact on Transatlantic Relations," Statement before the House Committee on Foreign Affairs presented to the 110th Cong., 1st sess. (Washington, D.C.: U.S. Government Printing Office, 2007), 8-9.

[63] Ibid., 8.

[64] Ibid., 11.

[65] Ibid., 8.

[66] Bush, *The National Security Strategy of the United States of America*, 8.

[67] Ibid., ii.

[68] David Cole and James X. Dempsey, *Terrorism and the Constitution: Sacrificing Civil Liberties in the Name of National Security* (New York: The New Press, 2002), 175.

[69] Ibid., 148.

[70] Ibid.

[71] Yoo, 18.

[72] Yoo, 16.

[73] Brzezinski, "Terrorized by the War on Terror."

[74] Ibid.

[75] Ibid.

[76] Ibid.

[77] Ibid.

[78] Eric A. Posner and Adrian Vermeule, *Terror in the Balance: Security, Liberty, and the Courts* (New York: Oxford University Press) 79.

[79] Koechler, 8.

[80] Ibid.

[81] Ibid.

[82] Posner and Vermeule, 59.

[83] Ibid., 79-82.

[84] Ibid., 155.

[85] Ibid.